GREAT
SCIENTISTS & INVENTORS

Albert Einstein

by Emily James

Pebble®
Plus

CAPSTONE PRESS
a capstone imprint

Pebble Plus is published by Capstone Press,
1710 Roe Crest Drive, North Mankato, Minnesota 56003
www.mycapstone.com

Library of Congress Cataloging-in-Publication Data
Names: James, Emily, 1983– author.
Title: Albert Einstein / by Emily James.
Description: North Mankato, Minnesota : Capstone Press, [2017] | Series:
Pebble plus. Great scientists and inventors | Audience: Ages 4–8. |
Audience: K to grade 3. | Includes bibliographical references and index.
Identifiers: LCCN 2016031959| ISBN 9781515738848 (library binding) |
ISBN 9781515738909 (pbk.) | ISBN 9781515739081 (ebook (pdf))
Subjects: LCSH: Einstein, Albert, 1879–1955—Juvenile literature. |
Physicists—Biography—Juvenile literature.
Classification: LCC QC16.E5 J354 2017 | DDC 530.092 [B] —dc23
LC record available at https://lccn.loc.gov/2016031959

Editorial Credits
Jaclyn Jaycox and Michelle Hasselius, editors; Jennifer Bergstrom, designer;
Jo Miller, media researcher; Steve Walker, production specialist

Photo Credits
Getty Images: Bettmann, 7, 13, 17, 21; Newscom: Glasshouse Images, cover, 1, Heritage Images/
Ann Ronan Picture Library, 5, 9, 15, Heritage Images/Oxford Science Archive, 19, Ken Welsh, 11

Design Elements: Shutterstock: aliraspberry, Charts and BG, mangpor2004, Ron and Joe,
sumkinn, Yurii Andreichyn

Note to Parents and Teachers

The Great Scientists and Inventors set supports national curriculum standards for
social studies related to people, places, and culture. This book describes and illustrates
the life of Albert Einstein. The images support early readers in understanding the text.
The repetition of words and phrases helps early readers learn new words. This book
also introduces early readers to subject-specific vocabulary words, which are defined
in the Glossary section. Early readers may need assistance to read some words and to
use the Table of Contents, Glossary, Read More, Internet Sites, Critical Thinking Using
the Common Core, and Index sections of the book.

Printed and bound in China.

PO7886LEOS17

Table of Contents

EARLY LIFE

Albert Einstein was born

in Germany in 1879.

As a child, Albert was shy.

He did not talk much.

Albert as a small child in the 1880s

Albert had many talents growing up. He played the violin. He was also good at math and science.

Albert continued playing violin as an adult.

Albert went to college in Switzerland. He studied physics and math. After college Albert worked in a patent office. A patent office helps inventors.

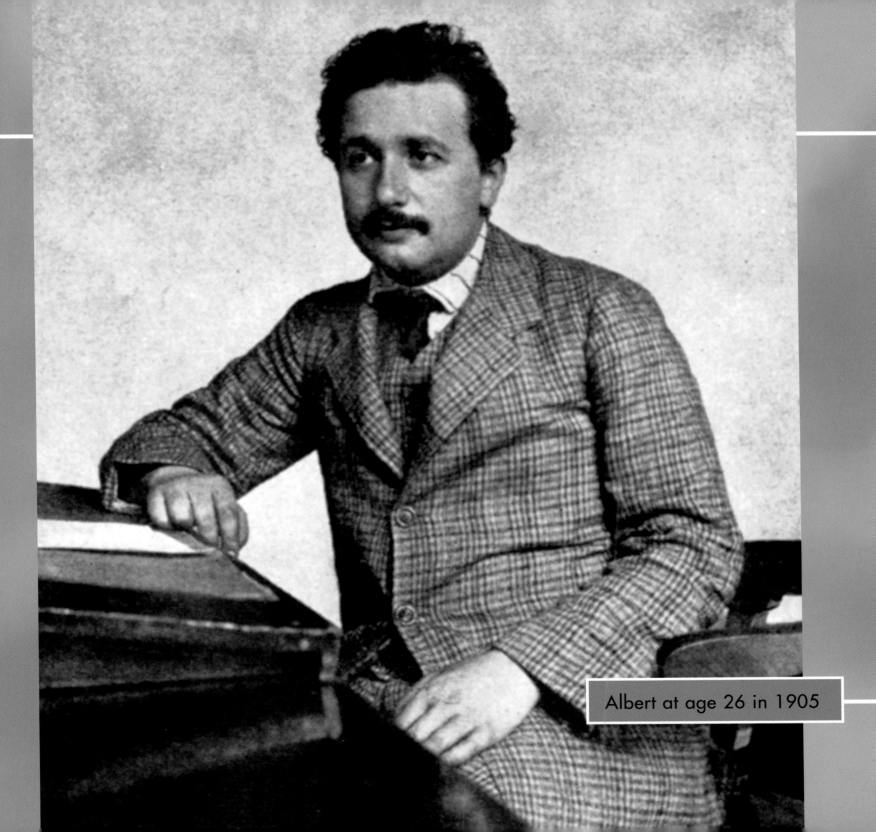

Albert at age 26 in 1905

LIFE'S WORK

In 1905 Albert wrote that
nothing moves faster than the
speed of light. This idea changed
the way people thought about
movement in the universe.

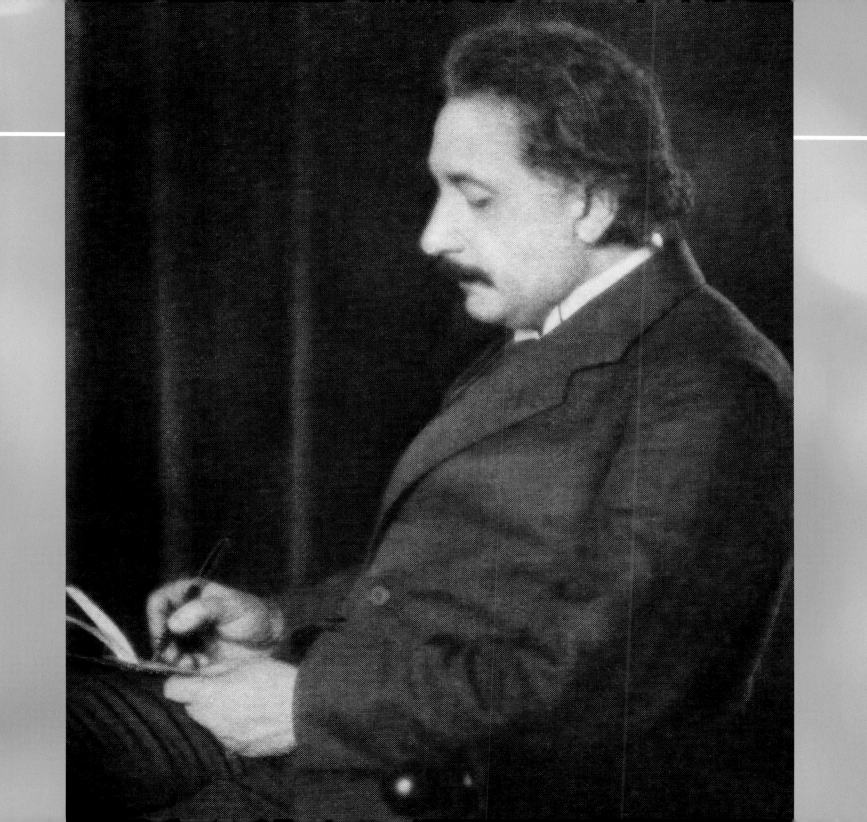

In 1916 Albert wrote about gravity. His ideas helped scientists understand time, space, and gravity. Albert became famous.

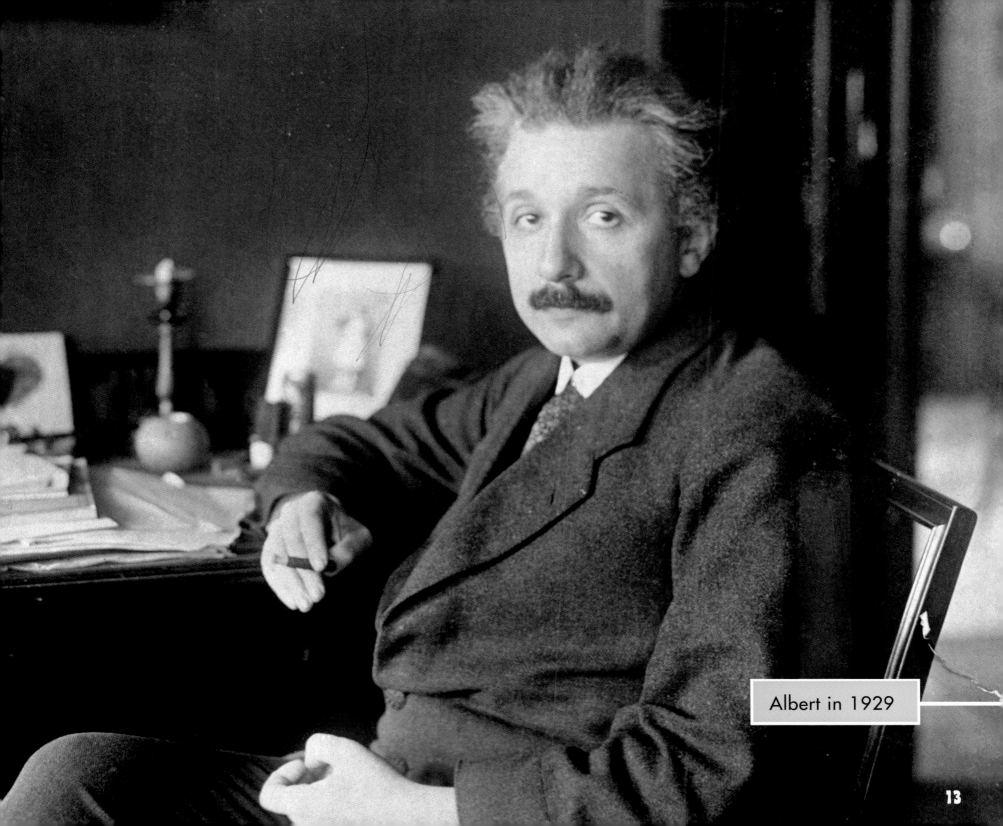

Albert in 1929

Albert also wrote about peace.

He spoke out against war.

Albert believed that fighting

was not a good way to

solve problems.

LATER YEARS

Albert traveled around Europe and the United States. He talked to people about his ideas. In 1921 Albert won the Nobel Prize in Physics.

Albert Einstein

Albert and other Nobel Prize winners at the Hotel Roosevelt in 1933

In 1933 Albert moved to

Princeton, New Jersey.

He taught physics classes.

Albert also worked on

science experiments.

Albert with one of his students

Albert died in 1955.

He is known as one of the

greatest scientists of all time.

Albert's ideas changed how

people see the universe.

Albert at his home in Princeton, New Jersey in 1950

Glossary

experiment—a scientific test to find out how something works

gravity—a force that pulls objects together

Nobel Prize—an award given to a person who makes a great contribution to the world

patent—a legal paper that gives an inventor the right to make and sell an item

physics—the science that deals with matter and energy; physics includes the study of light, heat, sound, electricity, motion, and force

speed of light—the rate at which light moves; light moves at 186,000 miles (299,338 kilometers) per second

universe—the planets, the stars, and all items in space

Read More

Berne, Jennifer. *On a Beam of Light: A Story of Albert Einstein.* San Francisco: Chronicle Books, 2013.

Gordon, Fernando. *Albert Einstein.* Scientists at Work. Minneapolis: Abdo Publishing, 2017.

Meltzer, Brad. *I Am Albert Einstein.* Ordinary People Change the World. New York: Penguin Group, 2014.

Internet Sites

FactHound offers a safe, fun way to find Internet sites related to this book. All of the sites on FactHound have been researched by our staff.

Here's all you do:

Visit *www.facthound.com*

Type in this code: 9781515738848

Check out projects, games and lots more at
www.capstonekids.com

Critical Thinking
Using the Common Core

1. Name two things Albert liked doing as a child. (Key Ideas and Details)

2. Why did Albert write about peace and speak out against war? (Key Ideas and Details)

3. Albert won the Nobel Prize in Physics in 1921. What is the Nobel Prize? (Craft and Structure)

Index